Gustavus Adolphus: The Life and Legacy of Sweden's Most Famous King

By Charles River Editors

About Charles River Editors

Charles River Editors is a boutique digital publishing company, specializing in bringing history back to life with educational and engaging books on a wide range of topics. Keep up to date with our new and free offerings with this 5 second sign up on our weekly mailing list, and visit Our Kindle Author Page to see other recently published Kindle titles.

We make these books for you and always want to know our readers' opinions, so we encourage you to leave reviews and look forward to publishing new and exciting titles each week.

Introduction

An engraving of Gustavus Adolphus

Gustavus Adolphus

"I had carefully learned to understand, about that experience which I could have upon things of rule, how fortune is failing or great, subject to such rule in common, so that otherwise I would have had scant reason to desire such a rule, had I not found myself obliged to it through God's bidding and nature. Now it was of my acquaintance, that inasmuch as God had let me be born a prince, such as I then am born, then my good and my destruction were knotted into one with the common good; for every reason then, it was now my promise that I should take great pains about their well-being and good governance and management, and thereabout bear close concern." – Gustavus Adolphus

"Read over and over again the campaigns of Alexander, Hannibal, Caesar, Gustavus, Turenne, Eugene, and Frederic," reads an excerpt from one of Napoleon's memoirs. "This is the only way to become a great general and master the secrets of the art of war." The "Gustavus" in question is none other than King Gustav II Adolf, widely remembered by the Latinized version of his name, Gustavus Adolphus. Some hailed him as the "Lion of the North," others called him the "Golden King," and a few knew him by the affectionate nickname "Hook-nose." Today, Swedish, Finland, and Estonian citizens alike continue to celebrate Gustavus Adolphus Day on the 6th of

November each year, topping off the flag day with special cakes garnished with chocolates that featured his likeness.

But who exactly was Gustavus Adolphus the Great, and why does Sweden continue to hold him in such prominence today? *Gustavus Adolphus: The Life and Legacy of Sweden's Most Famous King* explores the early life of the Swedish king, his ascension to power, and his greatest achievements, as well as the revolutionary military tactics he used to shape modern warfare

The Rise of the Golden King

"The devil is very near at hand to those who, like monarchs, are accountable to none but God for their actions." – attributed to Gustavus Adolphus

When the month of November rolls around the corner, it is not uncommon to see winding queues upon queues of families and loved ones spilling out of the front doors of Swedish pastry shops. The toasty warmth and delicious fragrance of freshly baked goods drifting out of the local konditori are often enough to keep these places packed, but on the 6th of this month, they are especially astir. The display windows are filled with a colorful and mouthwatering medley of cakes and treats in all shapes and sizes, such as the princesstarta (princess cake), yellow spongecake set upon jam or vanilla custard and coated with a light green marzipan and a pink sugar rose; kannelbulle, or cinnamon rolls either dusted with crushed almonds or drenched in icing; or the semlor, almond paste filling sandwiched between puffy buns.

But on that day, the star of the show is a divine local delicacy known as the Gustavus Adolphus pastry, typically a square slice of spongecake layered upon berries, lemon, or custard. Sitting atop a dollop of cream is a chocolate medallion shaped in the profile of whom the locals call King Gustaf II Adolfs.

It comes as no surprise to those who know its history that these pastries originated in Gothenburg. For starters, apart from its tapestry of history, Gothenburg, the second-largest city in Sweden today, is famed for its magnificent culinary scene, so much so that as of 2015, the seafood connoisseurs racked up a total of 6 Michelin stars. It was also, after all, founded by Gustavus Adolphus himself.

Most historians link the creation of this pastry to Gothenburg's unveiling of the Gustav II Adolf Statue in 1854. Near the Gustaf Adolfs torg (Gustavus Adolphus Square), where the statue was erected, the salons of the Bloms Hotel hosted "dessert exhibitions" showcasing delightful confectionery from the finest local talents. An excerpt from the Christmas edition of the *Göteborgs Handels-och Sjöfartstidning* reads: "There are articles here, which can be called called real, small artworks of their kind, such as small statues of Gustav Adolfsstadiet, medallions containing copies of famous gene artifacts made in chocolate and sugar, etc."

The statue

Sweets featuring the likeness of the king were nothing new. Plenty of publications in the early 19th century present advertisements touting candies, such as caramels, with the king's face delicately carved onto them.

The pastries that Swedes eat today did not become commonplace until November of 1909, when Carl Bräutigam of the Bräutigams Patisserie introduced the treat to the masses. Bräutigam, a patriot at heart, was stimulated by the German tradition of baking special pastries on the feast day of patron saints, and wished to pay homage to whom many consider one of, if not the greatest Swedish monarch of all time. When the pastry made its debut, the squares of sugar cake were served with lemon or chocolate cream, and was topped with a "royal pink rose bouquet." Only a few years later were the King Gustavus chocolates added. Nowadays, the pastry consists of ingredients typically found in 17th century Sweden: eggs, flour, butter, sugar, milk, and cream.

The 6th of November is nationally regarded as an official flag day. The Swedish flag, a vibrant Scandinavian cross in gold stretching across a field of blue, is flown at full-mast on every public building and flagpole as a tribute to the fallen king. Previously, November 6, the anniversary of the courageous Gustavus's death, was commemorated with riveting speeches and elaborate torchlight processions.

It was in Gothenburg that these rituals were popularized upon the 200th anniversary of Gustavus's death in 1832, followed by cities that were either founded by or had received notable donations to its local universities from the crown. Neighboring nation Finland, which was part of the Swedish kingdom for 7 centuries, refer to the occasion as *"Svenska dagen,"* or "Finnish Swedish Heritage Day"; Estonia, which was also formerly part of Sweden, also takes part in the celebration, known to the natives as *"Gustav Adolfi päev." Sjättenovembervägen,* or "Sixth November Road," found on the Göta highway in Stockholm's Älvsjö, was also named for the same purpose.

But why, in a kingdom with over 70 known monarchs, is Gustavus Adolphus placed on such an unparalleled pedestal?

In 1572, Danish aristocrat and renowned astronomer Tycho Brahe experienced what many in his time dubbed a prophetic vision. To say that Brahe was eccentric would be a understatement; although the astronomer marketed himself as a man of science and made significant strides in the field, he was undoubtedly bizarre. The man whose genius fashioned the most precise star-mapping instruments available prior to the dawn of the telescope was the same man who hired a "psychic" dwarf as his court jester, kept an elk as a pet, and lost his nose in a duel with another Danish scholar over a mathematical formula.

Brahe

On the 11th of November that year, now remembered as "Tycho's Supernova," Brahe stumbled upon what he recorded in his journal as a "new and unusual star, surpassing the other stars in brilliancy...shining almost directly above [his] head." Brahe's observation of what scientists now believe were the traces of a supernova made such an indelible impression on him that it was supposedly the primary motivating factor behind his decision to pursue astronomy rather than law. The blindingly bright star not only cemented his passion for the field, but it was through this star that he predicted the fall of Catholic dominion, as well as the rise of an influential, lionhearted prince from Finland that would elevate Germany to prominence and unshackle the Protestants from papal authority. Brahe even estimated a timeframe for the reign of this sovereign-to-be: between the years of 1592 and 1632.

As it turns out, the Swedes later claimed, Brahe's predictions were astonishingly accurate, barring one crucial element. This powerful proponent of Protestantism was not from Finland, but from Stockholm, and it was none other than Gustav Adolf the Great.

Gustav Adolf, or as he is more commonly known, "Gustavus Adolphus," was born on December 9, 1594 to King Charles IX of Sweden and his consort, Queen Christina of Holstein-Gottorp. Even as an infant, it is fair to say that many had uncommonly high expectations of the prince. He was the grandson of the celebrated Gustav Vasa, "King Gustav I of Sweden" and the originator of the House of Vasa. More memorably, it was Vasa, upon his escape from captivity in Jutland, who liberated Sweden from what the locals deemed as the oppressive rule of "Christian the Tyrant," thereby establishing its independence from Denmark. It was also Vasa, a devout Christian who had been educated by a disciple of Martin Luther, who pledged to instill Protestantism into all of Sweden. In addition to a number of religious reforms instituted by Vasa, he decreed that all his Protestant subjects adhere to the following affirmation of faith: "To serve God by being obedient to His Law, and by loving Him above all else; to believe in Jesus Christ as our only Savior; to study and teach the word of God with zeal...and to observe the Ten Commandments..."

King Charles IX

King Gustav I

Regardless of Vasa's keen and committed efforts to disseminate Reformatory and Protestant ideals and urge his subjects to abide by them, his endeavors were met with some pushback. It was not until after his death that through his youngest son, Charles IX, the Swedish Church officially embraced the Lutheran Augsburg Confession of 1530 as its creed.

Along with successfully ingraining and reinforcing Lutheranism as the national religion, King Charles IX was often described as an exceptional governor. Though reports about his unappealing character – his volatile temper, brashness, and abrasive exterior, alongside other questionable practices and borderline tyrannical tendencies – were equally prevalent, he has also been credited with reviving the national economy. The same man whose reign was reportedly rife with "uninterrupted warfare," promoted the advancement of local metallurgical industries, and incorporating foreign talents into the workforce.

Some attribute his vengeful, brutal nature to his chaotic ascension to the throne. Following the demise of his brother, King John III, in November 1592, the crown, as per tradition, was set to be presented to Charles's nephew, Sigismund III Vasa of Poland. Bearing in mind that these developments surfaced amidst the height of the political and ideological struggle within the Christian sects, the Lutheran Charles found the prospect of a Roman Catholic king ruling Sweden drastically unconscionable. Charles proceeded to lead a successful campaign to depose

Sigismund before he was ultimately awarded the crown, which only led to further tension, resentment, and discord between the Roman Catholics and Protestants.

Charles's aggression was not only directed towards the Polish crown. In fact, he swooped in during the splintering of Russia, fighting for the rights to Ingria and Livonia, eventually resulting in the Polish-Swedish War and the Ingrian War, respectively. Then, towards the last year of his rule, his obsession with the province of Lappland, also known as "Laponia," located in the northern neck of Sweden, evolved into yet another war, this time with Denmark.

As a result, young Gustavus, through no fault of his own, was thrust into the midst of this hostile and turbulent atmosphere. Needless to say, his princely privileges and all the opulent comforts that came attached with it are hardly relatable, but even so, his childhood, especially for a royal, was far from the norm. It did not take long for Charles to take note of his son's strikingly astute and inquisitive mind. Fully aware of the tumultuous legacy Gustavus would one day receive, the king made an effort to maximize his son's boundless potential at the earliest opportunity.

While most other royals his age were scampering through endless castle gardens, the 5-year-old prince was tagging along on his father's business meetings and military campaigns. Charles had every intention of familiarizing the future king and fearless military commander in-the-making with the duties and responsibilities that would one day be expected from him. The small child would sit in an oversized chair next to his father, feet swinging underneath him, in the presence of soldiers and veterans of all ranks as they discussed matters.

Once the adults had wrapped up all matters on their agenda, the naturally curious boy grilled captains and generals, who had previously served in the wars against France and in the Low Countries, about the most efficient battle and siege strategies, and implored them to dissect the complex machinations of war to him. And as opposed to playing with wooden swords and fiddling with figures chiseled into the shape of knights and such, Gustavus was admiring the fleet of warships docked at the harbor. His favorite ship, as a child would so crudely put it, was the vessel outfitted with the most guns and cannons.

Gustavus, like other royal peers, was fortunate enough to be classically educated by the most elite scholars, academics, and church officials the kingdom had to offer. At the same time, Charles ensured that the budding sovereign was comprehensively schooled in the history and politics behind the art of war. One of the tutors appointed to him, Master John Skytte, had been employed as diplomat for over 9 years before settling for a secretarial post in Charles's government. It was Skytte who instructed Gustavus on the subjects of Latin and general history, and who illuminated to him the laws and legal system of Sweden. The royal chamberlain, Otto Van Morner, along with other former soldiers, government officials, and political persons of influence, coached him on the fields of weapons engineering and warfare tactics.

The mastery of a diverse set of languages was another skill imposed on him at a young age. As maintained by Count Axel Oxenstierna, who would later become Gustavus's closest confidante, the young prince supposedly mastered 7 languages by the age of 12 (or according to other sources, 16). Oxenstierna explained, "In [Gustavus's] youth, he obtained a thorough knowledge and perfect command of many foreign tongues, so that he spoke Latin, German, Dutch, French, and Italian like a native, understood Spanish, English, and Scotch, and had besides some notion of Polish and Russian." This was evidenced by the notes young Gustavus scribbled onto his notebooks and the margins of his textbooks, as well as his letters, which were written in different languages and showcased his ability to switch from one to the other with ease.

Oxenstierna

Clearly a highly gifted child, Gustavus was frequently found tucked away in the corner of the castle library, his nose buried in a book. Despite his zest for the battlefield, he was not so much a fan of chivalric romances, adventure books, or fiction in general. Instead, he was partial to political literature penned by the greats of European history. He dedicated at least an hour a day to read and reflect on the works of various political figures, but he most often found himself returning to the progressively worn copies of Grotian textbooks. Gustavus's veneration of the Dutch jurist, Hugo Grotius, most widely known for planting the seeds of modern international law, would last into adulthood. In fact, it was Grotius' works, most significantly his 3-volume treatise, *The Law of War and Peace*, that Gustavus would later regularly consult, and it played a hand in molding his political views. In a nutshell, *The Law of War and Peace* examines "a system of principles of natural law" devised by Grotius, to be followed by those around the globe, irrespective of creed, social norms, and local customs. As asserted by Grotius in the treatise, it was the right of any one nation to trade with whatever other land it desired, as it was to defend the right in question, even through the agency of violence. Grotius' support of the sea as international territory is a recurring theme in many of his works, primarily *Mare Liberum*, published in Latin by Grotius in 1609. It was another one of Gustavus's favorites.

Grotius

The scenarios in *Mare Liberum* were directly lifted from the Dutch Revolt and the Dutch-Portuguese War, the latter a turf war between the Dutch East and West India Companies and the Portuguese empire. Grotius, advocating on behalf of the former, strove to disprove what he thought to be Portugal's groundless claims of possession over the open waters. Papal backing was not sufficient enough reason to defend such a claim, insisted Grotius, nor were the Treaties of Tordesillas and Saragossa, pacts signed by Spanish and Portuguese authorities that drew a demarcation line between the empires. Those pacts distinctly identified the lands and seas that fell under the empires' territories. Instead, Grotius urged all monarchs and leaders to disregard the status quo, remaining firm that it was "lawful for any nation to go to any other and to trade with it." Perhaps unsurprisingly, the Roman Catholics took immediate offense to Grotius' words, including his failure to refer to the popes by their proper titles, and considered them not only an act of overt defiance, but a thinly-veiled attack against the Church. The book aroused such controversy within the Catholic community that it was added to the Papal Index, a list of literature banned by the Church, in 1626.

Gustavus's thirst for military history was also quenched by the works of the 4th century BCE Greek philosopher Xenophon. Indeed, Gustavus was such a fan of Xenophon that he supposedly insisted he knew of "no writer better than he for a true military historian" on multiple occasions.

King Charles appreciated what he thought to be his son's healthy fixation with military and political history, but he also made sure Gustavus was athletically trained and rigorously primed for the battlefield, because the probability of war seemed to be growing greater with each passing day. Gustavus was made to take lessons in riding, fencing, and other knightly sports, and the clever and competent child excelled in each one of them. Somehow, the young prince also managed to squeeze music lessons into his crowded schedule, later developing a proficiency in the organ, amongst other instruments.

Gustavus's dutiful presence in the council meetings spearheaded by his father continued into his teenage years. Showing more shrewdness and perception with each meeting, the young man, even at the age of 10, began to insert his own opinions into conversation with great confidence. Still, it appeared that Charles, conscious of his own shortcomings, made certain that Gustavus's conviction and assertiveness would always be balanced out by compassion, humility, and steadfast loyalty to the Lord. In a letter addressed to Gustavus, Charles reminded him, "Before all things, fear God before all, honor thy father and mother, be tender to thy sisters, love those who have served me faithfully, reward them according to their deserts, be gracious to thy subjects, punish the evil, trust all men fairly, but only entirely when thou hast learnt to know them...Invade no man's privileges, provided they clash not with the law; diminish not thy regal possessions in favor of any man, except thou art sure that he will recognize the benefit and do thee good service in return..."

In the hopes of fortifying his sense of responsibility and enhancing his hands-on experience, Gustavus was even entrusted with assignments of his own. By the age of 13, he was analyzing actual petitions and being quizzed on the proper response to them. A year later, Gustavus was chaperoned by his mother to the southern sector of the kingdom for the first time, where he was to handle business on behalf of his father. Before their departure, Gustavus was blessed with more words of wisdom from Charles. "Receive with kindness those who seek your support, for the fear they may quit you in despair," prompted the king. "If you receive complaints from your subjects, you should sustain them each in his rights, so far as it may be in your power. So conduct that your governors and your provosts will follow your example, and God will come in aid of your efforts."

The following year, in 1610, 15-year-old Gustavus was presiding over the duchy of Västmanland. Gustavus alone went on to install the Riksdag – the supreme legislative body of Sweden – in the city of Örebro. At this point, membership of the Riksdag had already been revised by his grandfather to include representatives from 4 chief "social estates": the aristocracy, the clergy, the burghers (property-owning merchants, businessmen, and other commoners), and the yeomanry, or land-owning farmers.

Charles's rising absences were unintentional - his health was swiftly failing him. In mid-August of the same year, Gustavus made his first speech to the Riksens stånder (Riksdag of the Estates), but was forced to prematurely disband the assembly upon receiving word of his father's debilitating stroke, which crippled the king's capacities for the rest of his life. When it was determined that Charles was no longer fit to reign unaided, his 15-year-old son was made his co-regent.

While Gustavus was vested with more power and responsibilities than just about anyone, those who knew him attested to the prince's liberality and benevolence, which were apparently also far beyond his years. These traits, many biographers are quick to point out, were not inherited from his parents. His mother, Christina, was just as, if not more irascible than Charles. She was stubborn, harbored a compulsion for order, and was known to harshly hector her ladies-in-waiting whenever they failed to meet her impossible standards or fell short of the inflexible schedule she had designed for them. In contrast, the young Gustavus was a gentle spirit, and he treated servants, subjects, foreigners, and even captured foes with leniency and objectivity. One of the only ways to provoke the wrath of the otherwise even-tempered child was to speak ill of the Bible or Protestant ideologies. The sensitive and God-fearing Gustavus also showed zero tolerance towards obscenities and rude behavior, and he was not amused by jokes and stunts – even when made in jest – that poked fun at his deity.

Christina

To alleviate the pressure of the monumental burdens that awaited him, as well as to cope with his father's undeniably declining health, Gustavus devoted more and more of his reading time to studying the Bible. The teenager quoted Scripture, subtly wove Biblical messages into the instructions he bestowed upon his underlings, and encouraged them to live and work as if under constant surveillance from "the eye of God." "God has given me the crown, not that I should fear or remain in repose," Gustavas would later say. "Not that I should fear or remain in repose, but that I may consecrate my life to His glory and to the good of my subjects."

Even so, the teenager, having been made to observe from the sidelines what he thought to be the adrenaline-fueled excitement of war all throughout his childhood, became growingly restless. When the lessons and obstacle courses engineered for him by his chivalric tutors no longer posed a challenge to him, he began searching for a new trial to conquer, and he was desperate to prove his patriotism on the battlefield. Shortly after he was appointed co-regent, Gustavus proposed for his father to assemble a band of troops that he would captain in the upcoming Ingrian War, but to this, Charles refused, opting to delegate the responsibility to "other hands and older heads" instead. Gustavus was crushed by his father's seeming lack of faith in his abilities, but taking heed of the Ten Commandments, he honored – albeit with some bitterness – his father's wishes and decided against broaching the subject again. But rather than sulk or rebel, Gustavus took it upon himself to further self-educate himself in warfare and military tactics by spending longer hours in the library and soliciting seasoned combat generals and officers for their advice. A government official would later remark, "He [seemed] more occupied in ruling his kingdom, than with the ordinary pleasures of youth..."

It was only in 1611, at the height of the battle with Denmark, that the freshly knighted Gustavus was finally admitted by his father into the arena of war. Mounting his prized gray stallion, Gustavus galloped into Västergötland (West Gothland) and mobilized the troops stationed at their winter camps, even managing to round up a healthy number of foreign soldiers. From Västergötland, the troops, headed by Gustavus, marched towards the city of Jönköping in the province of Småland, where he was to convene with Charles's army at a predetermined location. The consolidated forces, ushered by the formidable father-and-son team, then proceeded south to Kalmar, whose diocese was one of the main divisions of the Evangelical Lutheran Church of Sweden, and delivered the city's inhabitants from the violence and oppression of the Danish soldiers. Charles was more than impressed with his son's natural prowess as a fighter, and he lavishly commended Gustavus for his bravery and decisiveness, even in the face of danger.

In hindsight, many believe that the ailing Charles had sensed that the end was near, and as such, needed to know that his legacy would be properly preserved by his successor. Only after Gustavus had surpassed his final test – his laudable leadership of the troops from Västergötland – did Charles feel at ease enough to succumb. Charles passed away on a gloomy Sunday morning, October 30, 1611, sending an already unruly Sweden into further disarray. Gustavus, as instructed by his father, rose to the plate at once, but as he was 7 years short of the legal ruling age in Sweden, the *Riksdag* had no choice but to hold a series of meetings deliberating over the issue. Close to 2 months later, it was decided, based on Gustavus's years of active participation within the government, that the age requirement would be waived. Thus, on the 17th of December that same year, Gustavus, who turned 17 years old the day before, received the bejeweled and cross-ornamented crown destined for him at last.

The retinue Gustavus became heir to appeared remarkably optimistic about the new chapter that their new king would bring. Even a foreign ambassador who met with him not long after his coronation had only pleasant things to say about him. According to the ambassador, King Gustavus was "a man of high courage, though not revengeful...keen of intellect, watchful, and active; an excellent speaker; and courteous in his intercourse with all men; from a youth of such promise, great things are to be expected.

Early Heroics

"Gloria altissimo suorum refugio (Glory be to the All-highest, the refuge of his followers)." – official motto of Gustavus Adolphus, adopted in 1611 on the date of his coronation

The start of Gustavus's reign was anything but glamorous. The 1.5 million or so of his Swedish subjects were girdled by the enemies his overambitious father had made. Moreover, resolving the backlog of unfinished business left by the now-deceased Charles IX was more daunting than even Gustavus could have envisaged. The kingdom's foes, some boasting up to 14 times the manpower than the entire population of Sweden, were thrilled by the abrupt transition of power, which they assumed to be a harbinger of the kingdom's downfall.

To make matters worse, while Gustavus was granted possession of the Swedish crown, much of the nobility expressed their distaste for the decision, pointing to his age. Faced with a rapidly shrinking treasury, no thanks to his predecessor's constant war campaigns, Gustavus had no other alternative but to seek financial assistance from those in the upper echelons of Swedish society. To his dismay, he was met with much resistance, and he failed to secure any funding from the nobles, for they were convinced that the overrated young king, who had been tasked with more than even the most hardened sovereign could handle, would fall prey to the costly traps of war and further exhaust the already depleted treasury.

With that in mind, Gustavus, though slightly crestfallen, foresaw their reluctance. Knowing that his reign would be problematic, to say the least, without the Swedish aristocracy on his side, he bit his tongue and instead made them an offer that he knew they could not refuse. He suggested a recasting of his advisory council, and he vowed to staff it with qualified nobles with diplomatic backgrounds and plenty of governmental experience, whom he would confer with before making any major decisions. The nobility, in return, would guarantee to him their full support and financial backing, upon the king's request. To this, the nobility, pleasantly astounded by the king's accommodating proposal, accepted at once.

The steadily swelling support and approval from his subjects revived his spirits, but Gustavus's most salient quandary remained unsolved. The 17-year-old king, as dictated by his unnerving agenda, was expected to not only juggle these simultaneous wars, but to lead Sweden to victory in all 3 of them.

First on his plate was the Kalmar War, the name of the conflict between his kingdom and Denmark between the years of 1611 and 1613. The Kalmar War sprouted from a centuries-long dispute with the Danish over "supremacy in the Baltic," or more precisely, what was known as the *"Øresund,"* or the "Sound," for short. In the year 1429, the Danish monarchs claimed hold over the Sound, the coveted channel of water that serves as a border between Sweden and Zealand, the largest and most populated island on the Danish coast. The Swedes had been contesting the Danish possession of the strait, the shortest and most convenient route from the

Kattegat (the swathe of sea confined by Danish hinterlands and western Swedish provinces) for well over a century. Swedish authorities accused the Danish of unjustly controlling both shores, as well as reaping and taking the profits made from the tolls levied on passing ships.

For the Grotius-influenced Gustavus, it was a matter of principle. It was King Charles who resurrected the age-old feud with the Danish monarch, Christian IV, in 1610, when he made the bold attempt to move in on Finnmark, a golden goose on the Atlantic-White Sea trade route that had been providing the Danish crown with a large and lucrative supply of fish and furs. Following Charles's death, it was Gustavus who was left to pick up the pieces as the escalating tensions erupted into full-blown war.

King Christian IV of Denmark

Eager to assert his dominance with foreign powers, and hoping to prove his naysayers wrong at one fell swoop, Gustavus acted speedily and aggressively, and unfortunately, it would cost him. Vastly outnumbered and outgunned by the efficiently organized Danish troops, the Swedes struggled to defend themselves, let alone launch a victorious attack against the enemy. The Swedish port of Kalmar fell into Danish hands in the summer of 1611, just a few months after Christian's declaration of war. In May of 1612, the Danes captured the Älvsborg, or Elfsborg Fortress, which was constructed by the outlet of the Göta Älv River to defend the newly erected Gothenburg and the settlements surrounding it. Just as importantly, the Swedes' last Atlantic trading post followed suit.

It was at this stage that Gustavus grudgingly accepted defeat. In an effort to prevent further inexorable losses, the anxious king summoned his advisory council, and together, they began to brainstorm potential stipulations for a truce. Perhaps not surprisingly, King Christian, whose ego got a boost from the Danes' winning streak, had no plans to withdraw his fearsome troops just yet. Now that Christian had conquered Gustavus's feeble forces, he was certain that replicating their military efforts in other Swedish regions would be just as easy.

Fortunately for the Swedes, foreign powers became alarmed by Christian's belligerent campaigns. Motivated by the fear that the power-hungry monarch's antics would upset the valuable markets of Sweden and its neighbors, the Dutch, as well as other members of the Hanseatic League, agreed to assist the Swedish troops. It was only following this unwelcome revelation that the indignant King Christian ordered his soldiers to lower their weapons. Peace was not officially declared until January of 1613, when the bickering monarchs buried the hatchet with the Treaty of Knared. Though Sweden succeeded in securing maritime trading rights and was thenceforth exempt from all tolls when utilizing the Sound, the Swedes had to cough up a whopping sum of 1 million thaler (approximately $100 million USD today) to the Danish crown for the recovery of Älvsborg. This hefty debt was not paid off until 1619. Conversely, Denmark received possession of 2 forts, as well as an "overland trading route."

It was supposedly towards the end of the Swedish-Danish squabble that the plucky Gustavus encountered his first near-death experience. In the deathly frigid winter the year prior to the signing of the peace treaty, Gustavus and his men were stationed in the formerly Danish-owned Skåne, otherwise known as "Scania." It was here, in the village of Vä, the most inhabited settlement within the 24 Danish parishes, that Gustavus and his 3,000 men intended to recreate the anguish and torment inflicted upon them by Christian's troops when they mercilessly ravaged Västergötland and Småland. And that they did – the Swedish troops stampeded into Vä and set the village ablaze in an unexpected ambush. It did not take long for the Danish troops to locate Gustavus and his men, who eventually set up camp in Vittsjö of Skåne to regroup. But rather than pounce on the Swedish soldiers, the Danish generals remained patient – a virtue Gustavus had yet to learn – choosing strategically to exact their revenge in the wee hours of February 12th, 1612, when most of the camp lay asleep.

Early that morning, the Swedish camp awoke to the deafening blasts of gun and cannon fire. Just as the Danes had anticipated, the groggy Swedish soldiers leapt out of their tents in a start, and as they scrambled for their weapons, they were mowed down by the enemy forces. Luckily, Gustavus, along with most of his cortege, managed to escape from the melee and flee north, making their way towards Dragsån.

It was here that they chanced upon yet another stumbling block. The Danish-operated bridge over the river, their only hope of egress, was swarming with Danish guards. But with the enemy soldiers hot on their heels, Gustavus and his men could do nothing but tread across the flimsy sheet of ice that had formed on the surface of the frozen river. Their hearts no doubt pounding, the king's companions trotted over the ice cautiously, and in time, they alighted on the opposite river bank.

As experienced as he was with horses, the king had rarely, if ever, ridden on such dicey terrain. Nevertheless, the externally composed Gustavus followed in tow. Alas, he was halfway across when he heard the unmistakable snap of the ice cracking underneath him. Panicking, Gustavus lashed his stallion with his whip instinctively, but the sudden weight of its hooves sent them both crashing into the frosty water. In between mouthfuls of the filthy river water, the thrashing Gustavus tried to paddle himself to shore, but with every attempt at hauling himself out of the water, another slab of ice disintegrated. It would take the quick thinking and joint efforts of 2 soldiers, Thomas Larsson and Per Banér, to fish Gustavus out of the water. Regrettably, Gustavus's beloved stallion and childhood friend plunged deep into the icy abyss, never to be seen again.

The principles of Grotius and other like-minded thinkers were the bricks used to lay the foundations of Gustavus's foreign policy. On that premise, while these political pundits condemned the ownership of any body of water, citing violations on fair international etiquette, Gustavus went above and beyond to claim possession of the Baltic Sea, so much so that the motto, *Dominum maris Baltici* ("Dominate the Baltic Sea") was adopted for his enterprising campaigns.

Seeing how other nations had unabashedly exploited the seas over the years, Gustavus was adamant that it was up to him to decide what constituted "fair use" of the treasured Baltic Sea. It was through this angle that Gustavus rationalized Swedish involvement in the Ingrian War, the second of the stormy conflicts unwittingly fell heir to.

Following Sweden's humiliating losses in the Kalmar War, Gustavus knew that there was much he had to make up for if he wanted to restore the pitiful morale of his subjects. Once the treaty was sealed, Sweden proceeded into the next ongoing battle, and though the Swedes were given little to no time to reorganize themselves, Gustavus, now wiser from having completed his first war, learned much from his past errors.

Whereas Gustavus had been overly keen and impulsive in the Kalmar War, the Ingrian War, which lasted from 1611 to 1617, appeared to be a far more feasible feat. At this point in time, Russia was suffering from what they dubbed the "Smutnoye Vremya," or the "Time of Troubles." The discontinuance of the Rurik dynasty brought about peasant revolts, foreign intervention, and a slew of slippery hands swatting for the imperial crown, which led to instability, insecurity, and an overall weakening of the once dynamic and dominant state. Gustavus capitalized on the faltering state of the enemy empire. Swedish forces were dispatched to Novgorod, the second largest Russian city, and Ingria, the patch of land by the southernmost shore of the Gulf of Finland, and he instructed his forces to lay siege to these localities. Much to their annoyance, a thorough scouring of these areas found them markedly less populated, and their natural resources bordering on sparse. Even so, Gustavus ordered his men there to stay put, and he directed his attention towards hampering Russia's Baltic expansion.

Impeding Russia's nautical expansion aside, Gustavus kept an eye on Poland and its transparent attempts to usurp the Russian throne. While Poland's intrusion only added to Russia's fragility, Gustavus sought to stop the Poles with urgency, as they would only pose a fresh set of problems for Sweden in the future.

By tackling the Russian predicament with prudence and sagacity, Gustavus's competent leadership allowed Sweden to emerge triumphant. By the end of the war, Sweden had captured the provinces and fortresses of Ingria, Kexholm, and Karelia, which not only connected the Swedish-owned Finland to Estonia but reinforced Sweden's hegemony in the Baltic. The loss of these key regions ensured that Russia would be unable to access the Baltic for close to a century, and as the Swedes had predicted, this barred them from expanding any further than Lake Lagoda. As such, it eliminated much of the threat to Sweden.

Moreover, the Treaty of Stolbovo, ratified by the authorities from both parties, ensured that Russia would relinquish all previous claims made on Livonia and Estonia, cementing them as Swedish possessions. The near-bankrupt Russian government was also obliged to shell out 20,000 rubles (roughly $540,000 USD today) in installments. In return, Gustavus agreed to recognize Michael Romanov as the rightful tsar of Russia, and to cease all intervention in Russian government. Additionally, in exchange for the Swedes' right to plant trading posts in Moscow, Pskov, and Novgorod, the Russians were granted permission to do the same in the cities of Stockholm, Viborg, and Reval. Lastly, the right to free trade at normal tariff rates was extended to the Russians, and while it was not ideal to the Swedes, this clause allowed the Russians a chance to repair their dwindling economy.

In spite of the outcome, which played heavily in Sweden's favor, the overachieving Gustavus showed a hint of acrimony at the results. "I hope it will be hard for the Russians to jump across that creek," Gustavus mused to one of his advisers. Still, Sweden's victory could not have come at a more opportune time. The Swedes, who were growing increasingly skeptical about forgoing the age limit for Gustavus, could finally breathe a collective sigh of relief.

Off the field, the resuscitated morale and now steadily growing support for Gustavus enabled him to achieve a string of long-awaited reforms. Apart from encouraging immigration, which diversified and strengthened the local workforce, culture, and economy, as well as revamping the education system, Gustavus worked towards refining the legislative system to improve the symmetry between the powers of the parliament and the crown. The bulk of the revenue derived from the king's policies – in particular, the upswing in tax profits – was set aside to finance the burgeoning Swedish army.

One can only imagine just how much more Gustavus could have accomplished with his state reforms, had it not been for the third war that he had inherited. The Polish-Swedish War was a sequence of on-again, off-again disputes that transpired in 3 phases: between 1617 and 1618, 1621 and 1622, and finally, 1625 and 1629. Out of all the wars Sweden found itself embroiled in, the Polish-led vendetta against them was perhaps the most understandable. Polish King Sigismund III, the former sovereign of Sweden who had been ousted by none other than Charles IX in 1599, had hardly recovered from his inglorious deposition. With Charles unable to stop him now, Sigismund, who undervalued his erstwhile foe's adolescent successor, came forth to take another swing at reclaiming Sweden. Not one to back down from a challenge, Gustavus called him on his bluff and sent battalions to the Polish-operated Prussian and Livonian coasts, aiming to seize their ports and the rights to the rewarding tariffs attached to them.

King Sigismund III

The spate of Swedish victories in the Polish-Swedish wars sharpened Gustavus's Baltic ambitions. In 1621, the Swedes succeeded in inducing the surrender of what is now the Latvian capital, Riga, then the third largest industrial harbor city in Russia. 4 years later, the Swedes captured Livonia, and the year after that, they took the ports of Pillau, Memel, and Elbing. The final battle of the war, which occurred in Honigfelde in late June of 1629, ended with a Polish victory, but by then, the approval ratings for Sigismund were at an irreversible low. Sigismund's decision to take on Sweden had never been a popular one, and critics equated his rash actions to playing with fire, but their advice fell on deaf ears. By the summer of 1629, uprisings compelled Sigismund to finally listen to the cries for peace. On the 12th of September, Swedish and Polish authorities convened at the neutral grounds of Altmark, close to Danzig in the state of Brandenburg, and signed off on a ceasefire known as the "Truce of Altmark." On top of the classification of Livonian lands to the north of the River Dvina as Swedish property, Sweden was to keep hold of Elbing. Even better, Sweden was granted the right to a percentage of the duties collected from the Danzig trade and the retention of most of their captured ports, many of which produced profits that surpassed the annual income of all of Sweden. Furthermore, George William of Brandenburg allowed Gustavus to establish Swedish posts in Fischhausen, Memel, Pillau, and Lochstädt, while Brandenburg received the rights to the Swedish ports of Danziger Haupt, Marienburg, and the Grosse Werder.

As one might expect, women and men saw in Gustavus the most eligible of all bachelors. Gustavus seemed to have it all; he was an enlightened soul, both mentally and spiritually, strong-minded but fair, and a warrior as skilled as he was intrepid. His youth and dashing good looks also played a factor. As described by a visiting Dutchman, Gustavus was tall and broad-shouldered, with a "finely proportioned build...a fair complexion," and cream-blond hair, paired with a lush golden-blond beard to match. As the years progressed, his hair grew lighter and his beard fuller and more peppered with copper. Notwithstanding the time he spent on the field, he steadily packed on a few pounds, growing rounder with each passing year, but this being an appealing trait at the time, his line of admirers only grew longer. One of the only flaws ever mentioned about Gustavus was his nearsightedness, a defect that hindered his performance on the battlefield.

Of all the women who waltzed in and out of his life, Ebba Brahe was the only one he would never forget. Ebba was the only child of Magnus Brahe, a high-ranking official in the royal court, and Britta Stensdotter Leijonhuvud, a marriage relative of Gustavus's grandfather. In many ways, Ebba was Gustavus's first friend; the pair met as infants and grew up with one another on routine play dates arranged by Britta and Gustavus's mother Christina. The mothers had developed such a tight-knit bond that when Britta lay on her deathbed, she asked Christina to adopt Ebba. Queen Christina earnestly accepted this duty, and as she had vowed to her dying friend, she treated Ebba as if she were her own.

Ebba Brahe

Gustavus and Ebba quietly fostered romantic feelings for one another in their early teenage years, but the more Gustavus became enmeshed in his royal duties, the further they drifted apart. Only after the passing of Britta did the 18-year-old Gustavus and 15-year-old Ebba reunite for the first time in years. The flood of feelings that came surging back prompted Gustavus to profess his love for Ebba, and Gustavus was ecstatic when he learned that his feelings were reciprocated.

However, while Christina adored Ebba for her exemplary manners and intellect, she was outraged to hear of the relationship that had blossomed between them. For as sweet as Ebba was, her son deserved more than just a commoner. In fact, she went as far as telling her son that Ebba was a "distraction." And though Christina made it a point to refrain from meddling in her son's politics, the uncompromising mother made it her business to ensure that her son would be betrothed to a royal. She summoned them both and expressed her explicit objections against their relationship. When they continued to rendezvous behind her back, she forced upon Ebba a revised schedule that would keep her at a distance.

Inevitably, the star-crossed lovers were more determined than ever to stay together. They carved out time for one another and exchanged cryptic letters decipherable only to the other. At one point, Gustavus even appealed to and secured the permission of Ebba's father to take her hand, only to be struck by a bombshell from Ebba herself. Her rejection of his proposal came in the form of a self-deprecating letter in which Ebba deemed herself "unworthy" and pleaded for him to move on. Most chroniclers suspect that Christina was the primary cause of Ebba's cold feet. "He can't marry you," Christina supposedly barked at Ebba. "And besides, you'd be terribly unhappy as a queen...You'd have me to deal with – everyday." Gustavus begged Ebba to reconsider, but when it became clear that Ebba had made up her mind, he let go with a heavy heart.

The heartbroken Gustavus was driven into the arms of the raven-haired and bright-eyed Margareta Slots. Margareta, the daughter of an affluent Dutch trader by the name of Abraham Cabiljau, met the 21-year-old Gustavus in 1615 Pskov. Like most, Gustavus had an inexplicable attraction to forbidden fruit. Still, though Margareta was married to Russian soldier, Andries Sessandes, the pair continued to see one another. In 1616, just a few months after the death of Andries, who had fallen in battle, Gustavus and Margareta welcomed a son who would later become Count Gustav Gustavsson of Vasaborg.

Gustav Gustavsson

As the lust in their relationship reportedly outweighed their shared interests, their short-lived romance fizzled out later that year. The pair parted ways, but Gustavus continued to acknowledge their illegitimate son, paying child support until Gustav came of age.

Shortly after his split from Margareta, Gustavus, at long last caving in to his mother's relentless demands for a daughter-in-law, began his search for a Protestant bride. Employing his court officials as his matchmakers, he was soon acquainted with the 17-year-old Princess Maria Eleonora of Brandenburg. 4 years later, they were husband and wife.

Maria Eleonora

A portrait of Gustavus and Maria Eleonora

Maria Eleonora was a timeless beauty. With her high forehead, rosy complexion, and flowing, fair hair, she was often hailed as the "most beautiful queen in all of Europe." Born to John Sigismund, Elector of Brandenburg, and Duchess Anna of Prussia, with a solid Lutheran upbringing, Maria Eleonora appeared to tick off all the boxes on Christina's high standards. Though not formally educated, Maria Eleonora, a creative talent, was a stellar artist, embroiderer, and musician. The stunning Maria Eleonora also attracted her fair share of suitors, among them Adolph Friedrich of Mecklenburg and William of Orange.

While the pair, in Christina's eyes, seemed a perfect match, their union was still met with great opposition. Duke George William of Prussia, the brother of Maria Eleonora, was among the most vocal objectors, for he feared (rightly so) that their marriage would worsen relations with Poland, which at this point still controlled the coast of Prussia. Electress Anna had even written a letter on behalf of her son, addressed to Queen Christina. This union, warned Anna, was "prejudicial to Brandenburg's interests in view of the state of war existing between Sweden and Poland." She urged Christina to ignore her husband's approval of their union, for he was "so enfeebled in will by illness that he could be persuaded to agree to anything, even if it tended to the destruction of the country..."

Rather than cast doubt on the pair's unpopular union, Anna's reference to a potentially biased Swedish-Brandenburg relationship only strengthened Christina's approval of the marriage. She resumed her correspondence with Anna and gradually succeeded in persuading Anna to change her mind. Following the death of John Sigismund in 1619, George William was appointed Elector of Brandenburg. Presumably due to Swedish influence, Anna began to view her son's opposition towards the union as overly aggressive. Later that year, Gustavus was invited to Berlin, where, in the absence of George, who was handling business in Prussia, he met with Maria Eleonora and Anna.

Gustavus proposed to Maria Eleonora that very evening. Flagrantly disregarding her son's authority, Anna had Maria Eleonora smuggled out of Brandenburg and into Mecklenburg, where the princess boarded a Swedish ship and set sail for Kalmar. She eventually made it to Stockholm in late October of 1620, and in just a matter of weeks, she was walking down the aisle in a gorgeous porcelain-white, hand-stitched wedding dress from Hamburg, embroidered in blue.

Despite the fairy tale wedding, the pair had a rocky marriage. On top of Gustavus's alleged infidelities, Maria Eleonora, repeatedly depicted as "stupid, immature, and hysterical," frequently complained about her husband's absence.

Meanwhile, Ebba Brahe, supposedly Gustavus's one true love, went on to become the wife of the handsome Swedish statesman and soldier Jacob De la Gardie, to whom she bore 14 children, the majority of them boys. This has left many wondering what may have happened had Queen Christina allowed Gustavus and Ebba to wed.

The Father of Modern Warfare

Michael Manas' picture of a reenactor dressed as a Swedish soldier during Gustavus's reign

"You may earn salvation under my command, but hardly riches." – attributed to Gustavus Adolphus

Bolstered by the Swedish victories and well-received reforms, Gustavus shepherded the kingdom into the Stormaktstiden, or the "Great Power Era." This golden era was defined by the Swedish kingdom's territorial authority and power in the Great Baltic, which elevated it to prominence as one of the indomitable and most feared powers in all of Europe.

The Stormaktstiden gave rise to a bevy of dramatic changes in the nation. To start with, Sweden was home to roughly 1 million citizens at the break of the 17th century. A century later, the tremendous Swedish kingdom, discounting its territorial possessions, hosted 1.8 million inhabitants within the borders of old Sweden alone. Owing to Sweden's liberal immigration policies, the loss of soldiers from all the wars did little to damage its population. Be that as it may, the number of Swedish citizens still paled in comparison to those of the top European powers.

Sweden managed to retain its stature due to Gustavus's matchless diplomacy, as well as his management and multitasking skills that many historians credit with propelling Sweden to the front of the pack. Though entangled in the serpentine vines of war, the king made certain that he did not neglect his administrative responsibilities. As a matter of fact, most of his polices were underlain by martial motives.

For instance, in order to obtain a more detailed and factual profile of his subjects, Gustavus introduced a record-keeping database consisting of elaborate reports on the annual salaries, assets, and other details about every citizen and business, submitted to them by the clergy leaders of the local parishes. The council was then charged with sifting through these reports for potential sponsors that would assist in the funding of the wars.

While the Stormaktstiden is partly why King Gustavus continues to be so cherished to this day, his spectacular innovations would go on to alter the course of modern military history.

The predictable warfare tactics employed by most of Europe before the time of Gustavus was due for a much-needed update. Prior to the popularization of gunpowder, opposing armies, comprising parallel lines of archers and the javelin, pike, and sword-toting heavy infantry, marched forth and collided with one another on the battlefield. As such, much of the success of these traditional armies was contingent on their cavalry, which aimed to blindside the infantry, flank-first. The Swedish king is said to have been among the first to retire these antiquated methods, opting instead for a game plan that married the old with the new.

Firearm technology in the 1600s still left much to be desired. Gunpowder propelled artillery was an even more unexplored and novel invention. Having said that, the decision to invest in the artillery proved wise, for it allowed soldiers to attack enemies from a farther distance, and it made for more accurate shots. Soon, governments from near and far were purchasing barrels of gunpowder in droves. With everyone and their neighbor kitting their soldiers out with gunpowder-based weapons, spears, swords, and other weapons constructed out of raw materials were no longer practical. Even so, these new weapons were unwieldy, which inhibited the speed of the soldiers – all but Gustavus's men.

As opposed to relying on conscripted soldiers and mercenaries, Gustavus defied tradition by transforming his troops into a year-round, standing army. Conscripts and mercenaries were typically relieved from their service at a war's end, with most taking up odd and seasonal jobs until their next call to duty. Spotting the inefficiency in the shuffling of soldiers and general disorganization of these methods, Gustavus assembled a standing army that was routinely trained and uniformly drilled, even during the rare times of peace. As this was a full-time job, only those who sailed through physical examinations, background checks, and preliminary obstacle courses were selected for Gustavus's elite army. The plump and punctual paychecks they received at the end of each quarter further incentivized young Swedish men to enlist.

Furthermore, Gustavus decided against the usual phalanxes – a medley of musketeers and pikemen moving in close formation – and maximized the freedom of movement made possible by the innovations of gunpowder. Gustavus elected to piece together entire regiments composed of only musketeers.

The Swedish king had never been one to rely on cannons, for these bombards were bulky, difficult to maneuver, and becoming more of a disadvantage than otherwise on the battlefield. Gustavus much preferred lightweight, easily manageable weapons with paper (or combustible) cartridges, and as such, he decked out the Swedish soldiers with a sleek musket of his own design, one that not only eradicated the need for auxiliaries armed with only forked poles to support the old-fashioned muskets, but the one-faceted title of "gunner" itself. Gustavus inculcated in his men a method known as "volley fire." Plainly put, the concept revolves around the soldiers shooting in turns. When a regiment of musketeers approached a cluster of their enemies, those in the front row (the "first rank") dropped to their knees. The second rank crouched with a slight end of the knee. The third rank, positioned directly behind the second, remained upright, allowing all 3 ranks to fire concurrent shots. This ingenious tactic, which was soon mastered by the Swedish soldiers, allowed them to fire and reload their weapons at record-breaking rates – allegedly 3 times faster than their rivals – simplifying the conventional manual of arms from 160 movements to a mere 95.

It was also Gustavus who introduced the phenomenon of "combined arms," though this term was not coined until centuries later. Pike squares, which were conceived by the Old Swiss Confederacy in the 1400s, entailed approximately 100 pike-wielding soldiers arranged in 10x10 formation. The squares were dismissed as irrelevant by Gustavus, but rather than scrap the pikemen from his army altogether, he chose to sprinkle them into his regiments. Thus, each unit was outfitted with a ratio of about 5:1 musketeers to pikemen, allowing the unit to fire as they pleased while defending the infantry and keeping rival cavalry at bay. This arrangement also enabled the soldiers on horseback to weave in and out of the melee with ease, and to safety if needed.

Much of the Swedish army's dexterity on the field had to do with the stringent training enforced on the soldiers. Skill and valor alone were not enough for one to make the cut - above all, Gustavus valued the qualities of discipline, obedience, compassion, and a staunch devotion to the Lord. God, Gustavus insisted, was at the center of all their military expeditions. "Got mins us," or "God with us," was designated as the official army battle cry. When on the battlefront, Gustavus was also known to have repeated the following mantra: "Cum Deo et victricibus armis" ("With God and victorious weapons").

To make certain that his men, despite their bloodied hands, remained faithful and pious, Gustavus made the attendance of 2 daily worship services compulsory, and he imposed upon them a strict code of conduct. They were to never, in any way, shape, or form, inflict unnecessary harm, bodily or otherwise, on their enemies, especially the innocent citizens of seized or conquered villages, unless explicitly ordered to do so. Anyone who was found guilty of pillaging, torture, or rape was immediately sent to the gallows.

Gustavus was by no means a slipshod, easygoing commander, but his men respected him all the same. They were not only obligated to but aspired to achieve the resolute discipline he expected from his men. Gustavus ensured this through leading by example. He did more than just attend drill runs and worship services whenever he found time to spare; he, too, wore himself out digging trenches and lugging around blocks of rock during the construction of fortifications.

On top of everything, the Swedish soldiers appreciated Gustavus for regarding them as equals. Contrary to the norm, which saw cavalrymen, artillerists, and other specialists atop the hierarchy, Gustavus did not believe in ranking his men by importance. His insistence on "cross-training" his soldiers, yet another technique of his design, prevented any soldier from receiving preferential treatment, for they were equally trained in all fields of the craft, making them all worth the same. At the same time, through this training, foot soldiers, pikemen, and cavalrymen received extensive firearm training. This meant that a disarmed pikeman could easily snatch up a nearby musket and defend himself if the occasion called for it. Likewise, soldiers classically trained in artillery and foot combat were taught to ride horses. This reinforced the military's sense of unity, and it allowed them to fight more efficiently as a unit. Gustavus's ideas proved so effective that they were later replicated by a number of renowned generals, among them Napoleon Bonaparte.

Gustavus's lack of fear in venturing out of his comfort zone was yet another quality that distinguished him from other military leaders. He did just that in 1626 when he tried his hand at ship designing. The battleship of his dreams, which was to be christened the "*Vasa*" after his legendary grandfather, was spawned by his Baltic ambitions, and it would take over 2 years to complete.

The *Vasa* Gustavus envisioned would be the first in a line of premium Swedish-engineered warships. Equipped with the newest and most ominous weapons, these vessels were sure to blow any enemy ship out of the water, literally and figuratively. But as the old saying goes, everything in life comes in either a blessing or a lesson. As it turned out, Gustavus's insistence upon interfering every step of the way, excusing it as good management, resulted in the latter. This was a lesson to be learned, and an expensive one, at that. The average design of a 17th century warship came with a single deck of cannons posted on either side of the vessel. Originally, the *Vasa* was to be modeled after this conventional, fail-proof design. That was, until Gustavus learned of the new designs rolled out by the Poles, which were furnished with 2 decks of newly-released, top-of-the-line cannons. Refusing to be overshadowed by one of his most fierce competitors, Gustavus demanded the presence of his shipbuilders at once, and he subsequently ordered them to add an extra deck of cannons to the *Vasa*. The shipbuilders huddled around the table for a better look at the king's convoluted blueprints. If the shipbuilders could indeed bring his blueprints to fruition, the *Vasa* would be the mightiest ship that ever sailed the blue seas.

Sadly, the path of success was obstructed by one critical factor: physics. The shipbuilders wasted no time in voicing their doubts, and they informed Gustavus that the ballasts in his design were nowhere near dense enough to shore up 2 hefty cannon decks. As such, the instability it was certain to inflict upon the ship would render it unfit for the waters.

Unfortunately, there was no changing his mind. When construction of the *Vasa* was completed in the summer of 1628, the vessel was primed for a series of safety tests. While the ship passed leakage and operational checks with flying colors, it failed miserably when it came time for the stability test. A crew of 30 sailors assigned to the ship was tasked with running from one side to the other to evaluate the strength and balance of the ship. Just a few minutes into the test, the groaning *Vasa* began to list, just as the shipbuilders predicted. The leaning was supposedly so severe that the crew was evacuated from the tilting ship at once.

By this point, one might assume that Gustavus finally swallowed the bitter pill and abandoned the project, but on the contrary, the obstinate king ordered the builders to make a few cosmetic changes to the wobbling decks. Against their better judgment, the builders did as they were told.

The *Vasa* was unveiled to the public for the first time on the 10th of August, 1628. The starry-eyed crowd that gathered to witness the historic event cheered thunderously as the vessel departed from the port, gliding across the temperamental blue-green water. Lamentably, less than a mile into their excursion, a billow of wind gusted past, tipping the ship to its side. Boats of ship engineers were dispatched to the scene immediately, but to no avail. The *Vasa* quickly became engulfed with water, and in effect, unsalvageable. A dejected Gustavus could do nothing but watch on helplessly as the sea lay claim to his precious ship.

An investigation was soon conducted to locate the source of the error. It was obvious to all that Gustavus was to blame, but since the king was infallible, authorities were forced to look the other way. Eventually, the sinking was written off as a mysterious "act of God," and the debacle was never discussed again.

A picture of the *Vasa* in a museum

As was the case with any female consort, Queen Maria Eleonora was expected to yield for her husband a male heir. The royal couple consummated their marriage on their wedding night, and less than a year later, Maria Eleonora delivered to Gustavus a baby girl. Unfortunately, she had no heartbeat. The couple mourned the loss of their baby girl, but they were determined to try again. As it turned out, it wasn't for another 2 years that Maria Eleonora was blessed with another daughter, and family tragedy had far from run its course. The couple was only afforded the company of their daughter, Christina (named after her grandmother), for a brief 11 months before she, too, was taken by illness.

In May 1625, Maria Eleonora became pregnant for the 3rd time. The pregnancy seemed to be on track for smooth sailing, until, ignoring the doctor's orders, an attention-seeking Maria Eleonora demanded to accompany her husband on one of his fleet inspection tours. The ship she boarded later capsized in a freak storm, and though she was rescued and safely towed to dry land, the traumatic experience triggered a premature birth. Their only son was born hours later, but alas, he, like his eldest sister, was stillborn.

The fourth time would end up being the charm. Maria Eleonora found herself with child again just a year after the loss of their son. On the 18th of December, Maria Eleonora underwent hours of excruciating labor, but the end result would make all the pain worthwhile. The midwives who assisted with the birth of their child deliberated for hours before announcing that the royals had produced a son. The newborn was coated with a "fleece" from head to toe, excluding its face, arms, and calves. What was more, the baby sported a head full of hair and had inherited Gustavus's masculine, hook-like nose.

Only days later did their blunder dawn on them. It was Gustavus's half-sister, Katharina, who approached the king with the shocking news that they had not produced a son, but another girl. Mercifully, whatever disappointment Gustavus had, if any, was fleeting. The king scooped his daughter, whom he would call "Christina Alexandra," into his arms and gently stroked her hair. "She is going to be clever," whispered the gleeful Gustavus. "For she has taken us all in..."

Gustavus's Death and Legacy

"The issue of battle is doubtful by reason of our sins, doubtful too is human life's span. I beg you, therefore, if it go hard with us, not to lose heart, but to look to my memory and the welfare of those dear to me...I have reigned for 20 years with grievous toil, but God be praised, with honor, too. I have honored my fatherland, and made light of life, riches, and good days for its sake." – Gustavus Adolphus, in a letter addressed to Count Axel Oxenstierna

Legend has it that the faith Gustavus had in God's protection was so strong that he declined to wear any armor, apart from a thin leather curaiss, whenever he charged into the battlefield. "I need no such thing," Gustavus gloated when questioned about the bold decision. "The Lord is my armor!" Most historians, however, have pointed out that his decision was most likely more motivated by necessity than it was by his trust in the Lord. The bullet fragments lodged in the muscle just above his shoulder, an injury he suffered in battle against the Poles in 1627, could not be extracted by any doctor, which likely prevented him from donning the traditional iron armor. Nevertheless, he still seemed indestructible.

The incident at Kalmar was hardly the only time Gustavus escaped death by the skin of his teeth. Yet even with the mounting number of lasting injuries, such as internal bleeding, pain from dislocated joints, and even a pair of permanently paralyzed fingers, Gustavus continued soldiering on. In May of 1627, Gustavus suffered a round of gunshot wounds during the Battle of Danzig, and just 3 months after that close call, during the Battle of Dirschau, the limping Gustavus was struck in his other shoulder by a sniper's musket ball, which missed his head by mere centimeters. His battered but resilient body was then giving one of its worst beatings 2 years later at the Battle of Trzciana. Not only was the king captured and held hostage – twice – by the Polish troops, he was smitten by yet another barrage of bullets. Yet again, he miraculously survived.

As fate would have it, Gustavus's luck would not last forever.

At the turn of the 1630s, the continent was upended by one of the bloodiest conflicts in its entire history, the religiously-charged Thirty Years' War. As committed to overthrowing the Catholic Church as they were, the Protestants had underestimated the military capabilities of their foes, and they suffered one brutal defeat after another. As such, they were in desperate need of assistance. The French chancellor, Cardinal Richelieu, elaborated on the situation: "All the princes of Germany injured and ravaged, looked toward the King of Sweden in their misery as navigators toward the port of safety."

Displaced Protestants flocked to Sweden for refuge. Learning of the plight of their Protestant brothers and sisters from the refugees, Gustavus called for a meeting at Upsala. There, the king took the podium, and before the expectant faces of the Swedish senate, he unloaded upon them the horrific abuses the persecuted Protestants were made to endure at the hands of the dreadful Catholics. It was the God-given duty of the Swedes, Gustavus declared, to save the German Protestants from the evils of their enemies. When his words were met with a chorus of muttering, Gustavus quickly reminded them of the consequences of a Catholic victory; not only would the progressively liberal Europe be swept back to the dark ages under the tyranny of the Church, Sweden was certain to lose control of its Baltic ports.

To make up for his prolonged absences at home, Gustavus rebranded his advisory council as a permanent cabinet, and he placed his officials in charge of all decision-making. Next, Gustavus dipped into the state treasury and collected donations, amassing a colossal total of 2,800,000 silver dalers. Once the preparations had been made, Gustavus summoned his officials to the Hall of Assembly and bade them farewell from behind the podium with his 4-year-old daughter perched on his good arm. "I've not thoughtlessly engaged in this perilous war which calls me far from you," he assured them. "Heaven is my witness that it is neither for my satisfaction, nor personal interests that I go into this conflict. Ready to sink under the weight of oppression which hangs over them, the German Protestants stretch suppliant hands to us. If it please God, we will give them aid and protection...I'm not ignorant of the dangers that await me; I have already been in many others, and by the grace of God, I have ever come happily out of them. But I feel that I may lose my life there, and this is why, before leaving you, I recommend you all to the protection of the omnipotent One...Farewell from the depths of my heart, and perhaps, forever."

With that, Gustavus boarded the royal ship, along with 15,000 soldiers and a fleet of over 30 warships and 200 transport vessels, and headed for Europe. These were the final instructions to his men: "Pray without ceasing. The more prayers, the more victories...Fear not the enemy that we are going to meet in battle; they are the same that you have already conquered in Russia...If you still show the same courage and perseverance, you will secure, to the Evangelical Church and to our brethren in Germany, the peace and security for which they are now suffering."

A depiction of Gustavus landing in Europe

The Battle of Breitenfeld in September of 1631, the first Protestant victory, was one of the most decisive moments of the war, and it is widely considered the crowning achievement of Gustavus's military career. Through his establishment of communication and supply lines at strategic points across the Baltic Sea, the securing of Protestant alliances, and his use of combined arms, amongst his other trademark techniques, the Swedish forces, against all odds, defeated their rivals. Such was the devastation inflicted upon their opponents that the Count of Tilly, the chief commander of the Catholic League's armies, had no other choice but to retreat. 6,000 or so Catholic soldiers were captured, many of them later incorporated into the Protestant forces. Whatever remained of the survivors vanished into the dark of the night.

Paintings depicting Gustavus at the battle

Ultimately, the climax of Gustavus's action-packed life was followed by a steep, plummeting decline. On the 6th of November, 1632, the Catholic and Protestant forces confronted each other once again on the elevated road leading to Leipzig. Duke Albrecht von Wallenstein, captain of the Catholic Bohemian troops, stood on one side, backed by a flurry of glowering faces behind him. On the other side stood King Gustavus, the Protestants' last hope.

Duke Albrecht von Wallenstein

About an hour after noon, Gustavus, half-blinded by the murky fog of smoke sweeping across the battlefield, found himself separated from his troops while leading a cavalry charge. Disoriented and vulnerable to his shortsightedness, the king wandered into the enemy lines. Before he could react, a bullet pierced into his arm, crushing his left arm and elbow. Gustavus whipped himself around at once, but just seconds later, another bullet whizzed past, striking his stallion in the neck. Growing increasingly numb by the second, he tried to steady his inconsolable horse but was knocked off by the sword of a passing cavalryman.

Blood might have been gushing out of his various bullet wounds, contaminating the grass with crimson, but his will to live was evidently unlike any other. When a breakaway squadron led by the Duke of Lauenburg found him minutes later, Gustavus mustered up the strength to ask his rescuers to remove him from the field. That said, as a page was dragging him towards the sidelines, Gustavus was finished off by another passing rider with a fatal shot to the temple. Even then, the king managed to squeeze out one final message with his dying breaths: "I am the King of Sweden! And this day, I seal with my blood the liberties and religion of the Swedish nation!" Gustavus had died at the height of another victory for his side at the Battle of Lützen, but his death would rock the Protestants.

A painting depicting Gustavus's death on the field

A depiction of the king's body being transported back to Sweden

The body of Gustavus's horse on display

For reasons unknown, the bullet-riddled body of Gustavus Adolphus would not be buried for another 2 years. Just as curiously, his widow requested for the removal of her husband's heart, which she kept for an unspecified amount of time before she agreed to surrender it to the authorities.

The king was finally laid to rest, along with his heart, on June 22, 1634 in Stockholm's Riddarholm Church. By then, the Swedish Estates of the Realm had awarded the fallen king the name of "Gustavus Adolphus Magnus," or "Gustavus Adolphus the Great." Gustavus remains the only Swedish monarch honored with such a title to this day.

Online Resources

Other books about Gustavus Adolphus on Amazon

Bibliography

Editors, S. S. (2012, November 6). Gustavus Adolphus. Retrieved January 11, 2018, from https://somethingswedish.wordpress.com/2012/11/06/gustavus-adolphus/

Trueman, C. N. (2015, March 25). Gustavus Adolphus – Domestic Policy. Retrieved January 11, 2018, from https://www.historylearningsite.co.uk/sweden-1611-to-1718/gustavus-adolphus-domestic-policy/

Roberts, M. (2017, November 15). Gustav II Adolf. Retrieved January 18, 2018, from https://www.britannica.com/biography/Gustav-II-Adolf

Editors, F. A. (2010, November 6). PASTRY ANARCHY. Retrieved January 18, 2018, from https://sierravegan.wordpress.com/2010/11/06/pastry-anarchy/

Editors, S. R. (2012, November 6). Gustav Adolfsdagen. Retrieved January 11, 2018, from http://swedenroots.blogspot.tw/2012/11/gustav-adolfsdagen.html

Editors, D. (2014). Gustav Adolfs-bakelsen. Retrieved January 11, 2018, from http://www.danskan.se/historia/gustav-adolf-bakelsens-historia

Editors, A. D. (2013). Gustavus Adolphus Day in Sweden. Retrieved January 11, 2018, from https://anydayguide.com/calendar/2681

Editors, A. A. (2011, November 7). It's Gustavus Adolphus Day/Anniversary of The Battle of Lützen. Retrieved January 11, 2018, from https://aminoapps.com/c/world-history/page/blog/its-gustavus-adolphus-day-anniversary-of-the-battle-of-lutzen/lZKp_jBIQuDRYWQ0m5ZWKDVeWXYGnZDlv7

Editors, D. H. (2014, May 5). Gustavus Adolphus – Early Life. Retrieved January 11, 2018, from http://discerninghistory.com/2014/05/gustavus-adolphus-early-life/

Editors, E. (2004). Gustavus II. Retrieved January 11, 2018, from http://www.encyclopedia.com/people/history/scandinavian-history-biographies/gustavus-ii

Wilson, S. (2012, December 2). The genius of Sweden's 'Lion of the North' . Retrieved January 11, 2018, from http://www.militaryhistoryonline.com/17thcentury/articles/geniusofsweden.aspx

McLaughlin, W. (2017, November 8). Gustavus Adolphus of Sweden – Fierce General and Master of Early Gunpowder Tactics. Retrieved January 11, 2018, from https://www.warhistoryonline.com/guns/gustavus-adolphus-sweden-master-early-gunpowder-tactics-mm.html

Vornicu, I. (2013, September 5). Gustavus Adolphus of Sweden (1594-1633). Retrieved January 11, 2018, from https://www.en.biography.name/leaders/58-sweden/83-gustavus-adolphus-of-sweden-1594-1633

Editors, E. D. (2008). Gustavus Adolphus. Retrieved January 11, 2018, from http://biography.edigg.com/Gustavus_Adolphus.shtml

Editors, R. S. (2012). Gustavus Adolphus - The Lion from the North. Retrieved January 11, 2018, from http://www.reformationsa.org/index.php/history/80-gustavusadolphus

Editors, E. B. (2011, November 11). Charles IX. Retrieved January 11, 2018, from https://www.britannica.com/biography/Charles-IX-king-of-Sweden

Editors, R. (2018, January 1). Charles IX of Sweden. Retrieved January 11, 2018, from https://www.revolvy.com/main/index.php?s=Charles%20IX%20of%20Sweden

Murray, J. (2013, Spring). The English-Language Military Historiography of Gustavus Adolphus in the Thirty Years' War, 1900-Present. Retrieved January 11, 2018, from http://www.wiu.edu/cas/history/wihr/pdfs/Murray-Military%20HistoriograpyVol5.pdf

Trueman, C. N. (2015, March 25). Gustavus Adolphus. Retrieved January 11, 2018, from https://www.historylearningsite.co.uk/sweden-1611-to-1718/gustavus-adolphus/

Trueman, C. N. (2011, December 19). Gustavus Adolphus and Sweden. Retrieved January 11, 2018, from https://www.historylearningsite.co.uk/the-thirty-years-war/gustavus-adolphus-and-sweden/

Editors, D. H. (2014, May 12). Gustavus Adolphus – Thirty Years War. Retrieved January 12, 2018, from http://discerninghistory.com/2014/05/gustavus-adolphus-thirty-years-war/

Mauler, M. (2006, August 10). Gustavus Adolphus Quotes. Retrieved January 12, 2018, from https://forums.civfanatics.com/threads/gustavus-adolphus-quotes.181666/

Editors, D. N. (2007). The Swedish Kings and God's name. Retrieved January 12, 2018, from http://www.divine-name.info/remarkable/swedishkings.htm

Anderson, J. (2010, September 8). King Gustavus's Folly: The Story of the Vasa. Retrieved January 12, 2018, from https://www.ribbonfarm.com/2010/09/08/king-gustavus-folly-the-story-of-the-vasa/

Hugo Grotius, The Rights of War and Peace (1901 ed.) [1625] (A. C. Campbell, Trans.). (2015). Retrieved January 12, 2018, from http://oll.libertyfund.org/titles/grotius-the-rights-of-war-and-peace-1901-ed

Editors, C. S. (2015, July 27). Hugo Grotius, The Law of War and Peace (1625). Retrieved January 12, 2018, from http://www.classicsofstrategy.com/2015/07/the-law-war-peace-grotius.html

O'Leary, M. (2015, May 8). Meet the Hip-Hop Pastry Shop of Sweden. Retrieved January 12, 2018, from https://munchies.vice.com/en_us/article/aey8yb/meet-the-hip-hop-pastry-shop-of-sweden

Editors, S. U. (2017, October 3). Cinnamon Bun Day - Kanelbullens dag. Retrieved January 12, 2018, from http://www.su.se/english/about/news-and-events/cinnamon-bun-day-kanelbullens-dag-1.5166

Editors, M. L. (2017, November 17). SWEDEN, KINGS. Retrieved January 12, 2018, from http://fmg.ac/Projects/MedLands/SWEDEN.htm

Wilkins, A. (2010, November 22). The crazy life and crazier death of Tycho Brahe, history's strangest astronomer. Retrieved January 12, 2018, from https://io9.gizmodo.com/5696469/the-crazy-life-and-crazier-death-of-tycho-brahe-historys-strangest-astronomer

Editors, R. (2004). The Observations of Tycho Brahe . Retrieved January 12, 2018, from http://www.pas.rochester.edu/~blackman/ast104/brahe10.html

Editors, S. (2011). SN 1572, Tycho's Supernova. Retrieved January 12, 2018, from http://spider.seds.org/spider/Vars/sn1572.html

Plant, D. (1995, Spring). Tycho Brahe: A King Amongst Astronomers. Retrieved January 12, 2018, from http://www.skyscript.co.uk/brahe.html

Editors, E. B. (2017, May 2). Gustav I Vasa. Retrieved January 15, 2018, from https://www.britannica.com/biography/Gustav-I-Vasa

Sampson, A. (2015). Swedish Monarchy – Gustav Vasa. Retrieved January 15, 2018, from http://www.sweden.org.za/swedish-monarchy-gustav-vasa.html

Editors, W. S. (2016, October 5). 1911 Encyclopædia Britannica/Charles IX. (King of Sweden). Retrieved January 15, 2018, from https://en.wikisource.org/wiki/1911_Encyclop%C3%A6dia_Britannica/Charles_IX._(King_of_Sweden)

Editors, N. W. (2015, December 16). Treaty of Tordesillas. Retrieved January 15, 2018, from http://www.newworldencyclopedia.org/entry/Treaty_of_Tordesillas

Editors, R. (2017, December 7). Riksdag . Retrieved January 15, 2018, from https://www.revolvy.com/main/index.php?s=Riksdag

Caballeros, D. (2014, January 9). Lion of the North and his Horses - Streiff. Retrieved January 15, 2018, from http://dariocaballeros.blogspot.tw/2014/01/lion-of-north-and-his-horses-streiff.html

Editors, H. H. (2013). War Matrix - Gustavus Adolphus. Retrieved January 15, 2018, from http://heihachi.eu/history/warmatrix/time3/time2/Gustavus%20Adolphus.html

Editors, S. R. (2011). Stormaktstidens Sverige 1611-1718. Retrieved January 15, 2018, from https://www.so-rummet.se/kategorier/historia/nya-tiden/stormaktstidens-sverige

Editors, C. R. (2017, January 18). "Lion of the North" Gustavus Adolphus and the Thirty Years' War: Fighting the Holy Roman Empire – Part I. Retrieved January 15, 2018, from http://www.camrea.org/2017/01/18/lion-of-the-north-gustavus-adolphus-and-the-thirty-years-war-fighting-the-holy-roman-empire-part-i/

Elkman, R. W. (2005, November). Stormaktstiden: När Sverige var som störst. Retrieved January 15, 2018, from http://popularhistoria.se/artiklar/tema-stormaktstiden-nar-sverige-var-som-storst

Editors, S. H. (2016). SWEDISH EMPIRE History of Sweden between 1611 - 1721. Retrieved January 15, 2018, from https://www.spottinghistory.com/historicalperiod/swedish-empire-sweden/

Trueman, C. N. (2015, March 25). Gustavus Adolphus – Foreign Policy. Retrieved January 15, 2018, from https://www.historylearningsite.co.uk/sweden-1611-to-1718/gustavus-adolphus-foreign-policy/

Editors, E. B. (2013, April 25). The Sound. Retrieved January 15, 2018, from https://www.britannica.com/place/The-Sound

Editors, I. S. (2016, November 4). Treaty of Knäred. Retrieved January 15, 2018, from https://ipfs.io/ipfs/QmXoypizjW3WknFiJnKLwHCnL72vedxjQkDDP1mXWo6uco/wiki/Treaty_of_Kn%C3%A4red.html

Editors, E. B. (2017, March 8). Treaty of Stolbovo. Retrieved January 15, 2018, from https://www.britannica.com/event/Treaty-of-Stolbovo

Smith, S. S. (2015, August 18). Gustavus Adolphus Revolutionized European Warfare. Retrieved January 15, 2018, from https://www.investors.com/news/management/leaders-and-success/gustavus-adolphus-father-of-modern-warfare/

Editors, R. (2011). Battle of Vittsjö . Retrieved January 15, 2018, from https://www.revolvy.com/main/index.php?s=Battle%20of%20Vittsj%C3%B6

Editors, M. M. (2011, November 6). Monarch Profile: King Gustavus Adolphus of Sweden. Retrieved January 15, 2018, from http://madmonarchist.blogspot.tw/2011/11/monarch-profile-king-gustavus-adolphus.html

Frage, A. (2015, May 30). Mr Fancy-pants and the silver throne – the life of a Swedish nobleman. Retrieved January 15, 2018, from https://annabelfrage.wordpress.com/2015/05/30/mr-fancy-pants-and-the-silver-throne-the-life-of-a-swedish-nobleman/

Editors, E. (2010). Margareta Slots. Retrieved January 15, 2018, from http://enacademic.com/dic.nsf/enwiki/11694207

Editors, H. R. (2017, November 25). Maria Eleonora of Brandenburg – A Queen on the loose. Retrieved January 15, 2018, from https://www.historyofroyalwomen.com/maria-eleonora-of-brandenburg/maria-eleonora-brandenburg-queen-loose/

Editors, M. M. (2011, September 12). Title: Maria Eleonore of Brandenburg. Retrieved January 15, 2018, from http://madmonarchs.guusbeltman.nl/madmonarchs/mariaeleonore/mariaeleonore_bio.htm

Editors, E. B. (2014, July 24). Kalmar War. Retrieved January 16, 2018, from https://www.britannica.com/event/Kalmar-War

Editors, S. H. (2002). ÄLVSBORG CASTLE. Retrieved January 16, 2018, from https://www.spottinghistory.com/view/846/alvsborg-castle/

Editors, R. (2017, July 2). Vä . Retrieved January 16, 2018, from https://www.revolvy.com/main/index.php?s=V%C3%A4&item_type=topic

Fernow, B. (2008). Charter of Privileges which Gustavus Adolphus Has Graciously Given by Letters Patent to the Newly Established Swedish South Company; June 14, 1626. Retrieved January 16, 2018, from http://avalon.law.yale.edu/17th_century/charter_014.asp

Editors, E. B. (2014, May 16). Time of Troubles. Retrieved January 16, 2018, from https://www.britannica.com/event/Time-of-Troubles

Rickard, J. (2007, July 28). Truce of Altmark, 12 September 1629. Retrieved January 16, 2018, from http://www.historyofwar.org/articles/truce_altmark.html

Editors, N. W. (2017). Gustavus Adolphus of Sweden. Retrieved January 16, 2018, from http://www.newworldencyclopedia.org/entry/Gustavus_Adolphus_of_Sweden#Biography

Editors, D. H. (2014, June 9). Gustavus Adolphus – Battle of Lützen. Retrieved January 16, 2018, from http://discerninghistory.com/2014/06/gustavus-adolphus-battle-of-lutzen/

Stevens, J. (2017). *Gustavus Adolphus*. Merkaba Press.

Grant, R. G. (2017). *1001 Battles That Changed the Course of History*. Book Sales.

Free Books by Charles River Editors

We have brand new titles available for free most days of the week. To see which of our titles are currently free, click on this link.

Discounted Books by Charles River Editors

We have titles at a discount price of just 99 cents everyday. To see which of our titles are currently 99 cents, click on this link.

Made in the USA
Middletown, DE
15 August 2019